Franklin D. Roosevelt

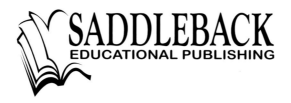

SADDLEBACK
EDUCATIONAL PUBLISHING

Saddleback's Graphic Biographies

Copyright © 2008 by Saddleback Educational Publishing

All rights reserved. No part of this book may be reproduced in any form or by any means, electronic or mechanical, including photocopying, recording, or by any information storage and retrieval system without the written permission of the publisher.

ISBN-13: 978-1-59905-222-9
ISBN-10: 1-59905-222-9
eBook: 978-1-60291-585-5

Printed in Guangzhou, China
0610/06-52-10

13 12 11 10   2 3 4 5 6 7 8 9

Franklin Roosevelt was called the most loved and the most hated American president since Abraham Lincoln. Like Lincoln, he had to hold the country together—first against the internal threat of economic disaster, then against the military dictators who wanted to make slaves of the free world.

Yesterday, December 7, 1941, a day that will live in infamy, the United States was attacked by the forces of the Empire of Japan.

The year was 1882. A doctor's buggy hurried to Springwood, an estate in Hyde Park, New York.

Good evening, sir.

The next morning, James Roosevelt wrote in a diary.

January 30, at quarter to nine, my Sallie had a splendid, large baby boy.

Soon the baby's mother was strong again.

Let me bathe him ma'am!

He is so plump and sweet, I want to do it myself.

In a few weeks he was christened* at the nearby chapel.

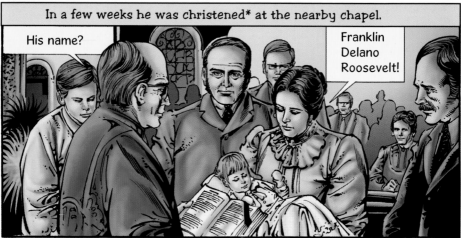

His name?

Franklin Delano Roosevelt!

* to give a name to at baptism

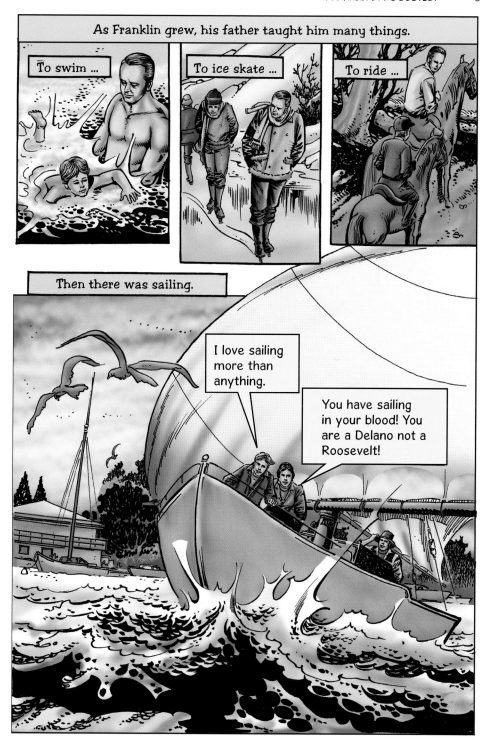

When I was eight years old I sailed to China on one of my father's sailing ships!

There were indoor things too ...

Read any books you find interesting!

Thank you. I like geography and history, especially naval history.

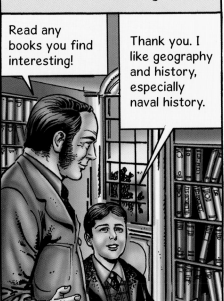

You get letters from all over the world. Could I start a collection of interesting stamps?

Of course!

For school he had a private teacher and had to follow a strict schedule.

Your winter schedule: up at seven, breakfast at eight, lessons from nine to twelve. Then outdoors for an hour of exercise, lunch, and lessons again until 4 o'clock.

Franklin had quite a few cousins around. One was Theodore Roosevelt.

Cousin Theodore has been made New York police commissioner. He's a very successful politician, too bad he's a Republican.

Maybe I'll go into politics someday.

Nonsense! Politics is no career for a gentleman.

At fourteen, Franklin was to go away to school.

Groton is the finest school in the country. We entered you the year it opened, when you were two years old.

They took trains to Massachusetts, then a carriage.

It's like a college campus.

We'll go first to the headmaster's office, Dr. Endicott Peabody. He is a fine educator.

Later they went to Franklin's room.

It's stricter than home! We start with a cold shower at 6:30, and end by dressing in evening clothes for dinner.

You'll like it when you are used to it.

Franklin's first report card was sent home.

His grades are very good!

And a special note from Dr. Peabody. "He strikes me as an intelligent and faithful scholar and a good boy."

The school year passed quickly. The boys began to talk about summer plans.

We have a summer place on Campobello Island up between Maine and Canada and a sailboat called the *Half-Moon*. It's super!

And soon it was summer.

All right, a hard to port!

HALF-MOON

After three years at Groton, he enrolled as a freshman at Harvard University in Cambridge, Massachusetts. It was 1900.

At Groton we were told what to do with every minute of time. Here, we make up our own minds.

I'll spend some of my spare time managing the freshman football team. How about you?

I want to be a reporter on the *Harvard Crimson* newspaper. That will take work.

And I'm joining the Harvard Republican Club. My cousin, Teddy Roosevelt, is the Republican candidate for vice president of the United States!

The Harvard students marched in a big parade.

I don't know what my father would say. He's a Democrat!

HARVARD WANTS McKINLEY AND ROOSEV

VOTE REPUBLICAN

McKinley and Roosevelt were elected. When McKinley was assassinated, Teddy Roosevelt became president. Then Franklin's father died. His mother moved to Boston to be near her son.

How are things at Harvard, dear?

My classes are going well. I go to lots of parties. And I've been chosen as a reporter for the *Harvard Crimson*.

But Franklin, have you been asked to join a good club?

I suppose I will be, Mama. But I've met lots of splendid fellows who don't even care about clubs.

Some of them have to work at part-time jobs just to eat while they attend school.

They hardly sound like the class of people you should choose for friends.

But Franklin kept on meeting and making friends with all sorts of people.

One holiday, Franklin traveled by train to Hyde Park.

Why, aren't you my cousin Eleanor?

Franklin Roosevelt! How nice to see you.

Mother is in the parlor car. Won't you come back and chat with her?

Certainly!

Eleanor Roosevelt, an orphan, was Franklin's fifth cousin. They had not met for several years.

Later ...

I've only just returned from three years at school in England. This winter I'll live with Aunt Edith in New York.

Of course, my dear!

I hope to see you there!

On weekends and holidays Franklin went to New York.

I don't really care much for dances and parties. I prefer my work at the Children's Aid Society and the settlement houses.

I admire that! I am just learning how many poor people there are who need help.

With other cousins, Eleanor visited at Hyde Park.

A hay-ride and a picnic, what a fine idea!

... and at Harvard.

What a shame, Harvard lost!

Next year as editor of the *Crimson*, I'll campaign for a better team and more student support for it!

In December 1903 ...

I am the luckiest man in the world. I have proposed to Eleanor, and she has accepted me!

I had no idea! You are both so young. You have plenty of time.

It will only mean that you will have two children to love you instead of one.

Eleanor is a dear girl. Perhaps if you wait awhile, go with me on a spring cruise.

They waited, but did not change their minds. They were married on March 17, 1905. Eleanor's uncle, President Teddy Roosevelt, gave the bride away.

This is one wedding where the bride is not the center of attention.

I like it that way!

On a honeymoon trip to Europe, they visited the Italian Alps ...

... and Venice.

It is more wonderful than I had imagined.

Nothing else could be so lovely!

At home again, Franklin entered a law firm in New York. They set up a household next to his mother, and soon there were two babies.

I would like to take care of Anna and Elliot myself.

Oh no, my dear! You must have a nurse for each child!

Franklin's mother still made most household decisions.

Then in 1910 ...

The New York Democrats want me to run for the state Senate. I'd like to, it's more of a public service job than my law practice.

They think it's a hopeless district for a Democrat, but I intend to win!

I hope you do, if that's what you want!

No Democrat had won in Dutchess County since 1856. But Franklin hired a red car and covered the county.

That's Franklin Roosevelt. Seems like a nice young fellow.

First time anybody campaigned from a car in New York State.

Franklin won by more than 1,000 votes.

They moved to Albany, the state capital. Their house was always full of politicians.

How do you stand it? And how do you ever manage?

I like it, I often join the talks! And I keep plenty of cheese and crackers on hand.

On her own for the first time, Eleanor was learning that she could manage very well.

In 1912 Franklin went as a delegate to the Democratic Convention to name a candidate for president.

He met Josephus Daniels there.

More than anything, I want to see Woodrow Wilson as president.

You are just the kind of young liberal we want on our side!

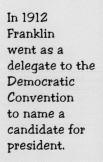

Wilson was elected. In Washington for the inauguration, Franklin met Daniels again.

I'm to be Wilson's secretary of the navy. How would you like to be my assistant?

It's the job I'd like above all others! I've loved ships and naval history all my life!

Fine! Make your arrangements to move to Washington.

He wanted to learn all about everything. He inspected navy yards and ships.

Mr. Secretary, we need to build up our navy!

I want that too. But Secretary Daniels and the president feel it might lead to war.

World War I began in Europe. Germany's submarines sank many ships, including American ships.

We do need a strong navy! But I am beginning to understand the president. It is terrible to have to send men to fight and die.

And each man is somebody's son.

By then, Roosevelt had four sons.

In 1917 President Wilson asked Congress to declare war against Germany.

The world must be made safe for democracy. We have no selfish ends to serve.

Wilson and other peace-loving people were determined to make it the last war.

Franklin and Eleanor were at the Paris Peace Conference that ended the war. Wilson presented a plan for peace which included a League of Nations.

The United States must join the League or it will never work!

But the United States turned away from Europe and refused to join. Roosevelt kept on fighting for the League.

At the 1920 Democratic Convention, James M. Cox of Ohio was nominated for president.

Who do you want for vice president, Mr. Cox?

Franklin D. Roosevelt of New York!

It was a big surprise. Everybody at the convention voted for Franklin.

I will make speeches all over the country to persuade the United States to join the League of Nations in its struggle for a peaceful world.

He made three trips across the country, speaking to people everywhere.

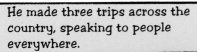

My friends ...

Some of the men with us think you will be president someday, Franklin.

1920 was a Republican year. The Democratic candidate lost. But Franklin became known all over the country.

The next summer the family gathered at Campobello.

It's my first real vacation since the war, I mean to enjoy it!

Then one night ...

I must have caught a cold, I ache all over.

You have a fever.

Soon Franklin could not move his legs. The doctor came. He sent for a specialist.

He has polio, infantile paralysis, it is called. We know so little about it.

Will he recover?

The amount of recovery depends mostly on the patient, his willpower, and his courage. He must not give up.

Franklin never gives up! And I will help him.

He went to a New York hospital. Then he was sent home. He could be lifted into a wheelchair, but his legs were useless. He was often in pain.

Louis Howe was Franklin's friend and political chief of staff. He talked with Eleanor and Franklin's mother.

The time has come for Franklin to give up politics and live at Hyde Park as a country gentleman.

It would kill him to give up! He could never live as an invalid.

I've said it over and over, he will be president someday. This polio makes no difference.

As for Franklin ...

I am not sick! I won't let anyone think of me as sick! And if my legs are weak, I'll build up the rest of me.

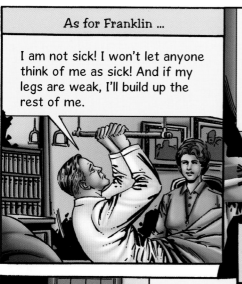

While Franklin recovers, you must keep the Roosevelt name before the public. Enter politics! Make speeches!

Me? Well, I'll try.

She overcame her shyness. She worked hard in Democratic politics. She learned to speak in public.

The doctors told Franklin to swim. Supported by water, he could exercise his legs. In 1924 he went to Warm Springs, Georgia.

There is feeling in my toes for the first time since my attack. I'll come here every winter until my legs are strong.

He started a group to turn Warm Springs into a treatment center for the crippled and handicapped.

He worked at a job. He was active again in politics. In 1928 he was elected governor of New York and returned to Albany.

In his second term as governor a terrible depression hit the country. Businesses failed. Millions of people were out of work and poor.

I am starting an emergency relief agency. Other states want to copy it.

Shouldn't the federal government do something? People are in trouble all over the country!

But Herbert Hoover, the Republican President, was against it.

I do not believe in direct relief. If Congress passes such a bill, I will not let it become law.

We must help banks, industries, big businesses. After a while that will help the working man.

But the working man was starving. He could not wait. Roosevelt made a speech.

We should build from the bottom up. We need plans that put faith in the forgotten man at the bottom of the economic ladder!

NBC CBS

In 1932 Roosevelt was the Democratic candidate for president.

Starving people stood in breadlines for food ...

Lived in shanty towns ...

Roamed the country looking for jobs ...

Roosevelt was elected. He spoke to the people.

This nation asks for action, and action now! Our greatest primary task is to put people to work.

He took action at once.

We must do something about the banks. I want a relief act to rush money to people who are starving. Let's pay jobless people to build things the country needs.

Within three months, fifteen new laws brought about big changes.

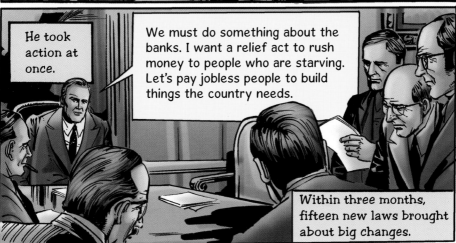

The "forgotten man" began to hope again.

Hey, I got a job today!

Oh, thank God! And thank FDR!

Young men were given a chance to live in camps, make money, and work at conservation projects.

College students could work to pay for their education.

I got much needed help. Plus you get enough hours of work to pay your tuition.

Not everyone was pleased.

With that man in the White House, we're headed straight for socialism!

And the taxes to pay for his schemes will ruin us.

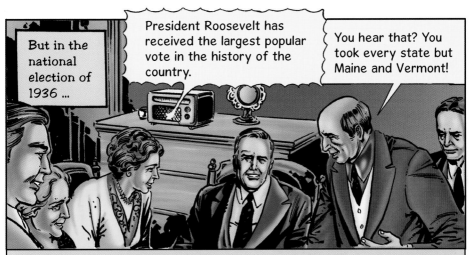

But in the national election of 1936 ...

President Roosevelt has received the largest popular vote in the history of the country.

You hear that? You took every state but Maine and Vermont!

But as things grew better in America, war raged in Europe. Austria, Czechoslovakia, and Poland fell to Hitler's powerful German army. Then Holland, Belgium, France ...

Bombs exploded ...

Paratroopers invaded ...

Fleeing civilians were machine-gunned from airplanes.

England was alone. German bombers came over in great waves.

In Washington ...

I hate war! The people of the country don't want war! But freedom is being threatened all over the world, and we'll be left to fight.

He announced a new idea.

We will not go to war. We will lend England the tools to fight with, as one would lend a hose to a neighbor to put out a threatening fire.

Early in 1941, he spelled out his long term goals for peace, the Four Freedoms.

Freedom of speech, freedom of worship, freedom from want, freedom from fear of aggression everywhere in the world!

Then, on December 7, the Pacific fleet at Pearl Harbor was attacked without warning by Japanese planes. The next morning he addressed Congress.

Yesterday, December 7, 1941, a day that will live in infamy, the United States was attacked by the forces of the Empire of Japan.

Congress quickly voted to declare war.

The whole country backed the President and the war effort.

Factories built planes and tanks instead of refrigerators and cars.

American soldiers fighting all over the world were typified by the four Roosevelt sons.

Elliot in the U.S. Air Force ...

James in the U.S. Marines ...

Franklin Jr. and John in the U.S. Navy ...

Eleanor took the president's greeting to men fighting in the South Pacific.

The president went to places like Casablanca, Yalta, and Tehran to meet with other world leaders.

And there were still politics and elections.

Everything in me cries out to go home to Hyde Park. But it is dangerous to change horses in midstream.

It would be hard for anyone else to take over in this crisis.

He was re-elected for a third term, and a fourth.

He never stopped planning for a peaceful world. In March 1945 he went to Warm Springs and dictated a speech.

The work, my friends, is peace. More than an end of this war—an end to the beginnings of all wars!

On April 12, as an artist painted his portrait, suddenly ...

I have a terrific headache.

He collapsed. A doctor came quickly. But four hours later Franklin Roosevelt was dead of a brain hemorrhage.

Eleanor flew to Warm Springs. Then once again, a funeral train carried the casket of a dead president across the country.

By his own wish, President Roosevelt's last resting place was in the rose garden at Hyde Park.

Franklin Roosevelt had come home at last.

the END

Saddleback's Graphic
Fiction & Nonfiction

If you enjoyed this Graphic Biography ... you will also
enjoy our other graphic titles including:

Graphic Classics

- Around the World in Eighty Days
- The Best of Poe
- Black Beauty
- The Call of the Wild
- A Christmas Carol
- A Connecticut Yankee in King Arthur's Court
- Dr. Jekyll and Mr. Hyde
- Dracula
- Frankenstein
- The Great Adventures of Sherlock Holmes
- Gulliver's Travels
- Huckleberry Finn
- The Hunchback of Notre Dame
- The Invisible Man
- Jane Eyre
- Journey to the Center of the Earth
- Kidnapped
- The Last of the Mohicans
- The Man in the Iron Mask
- Moby Dick
- The Mutiny On Board H.M.S. Bounty
- The Mysterious Island
- The Prince and the Pauper
- The Red Badge of Courage
- The Scarlet Letter
- The Swiss Family Robinson
- A Tale of Two Cities
- The Three Musketeers
- The Time Machine
- Tom Sawyer
- Treasure Island
- 20,000 Leagues Under the Sea
- The War of the Worlds

Graphic Shakespeare

- As You Like It
- Hamlet
- Julius Caesar
- King Lear
- Macbeth
- The Merchant of Venice
- A Midsummer Night's Dream
- Othello
- Romeo and Juliet
- The Taming of the Shrew
- The Tempest
- Twelfth Night

SADDLEBACK
EDUCATIONAL PUBLISHING